NEW JERUSALEM/EL RIO
HISTORY PROJECT

New Jerusalem/El Rio History Project

Ventura County's Holy Land

Mario A. Riley Sr.

Hosea 4: 6 People perish for lack of knowledge

PALMETTO
PUBLISHING
Charleston, SC
www.PalmettoPublishing.com

© 2024 by Mario A. Riley Sr.

All rights reserved.

This book or any portion thereof may not be reproduced or used in any manner whatsoever without the express written permission of the publisher except for the use of brief quotations in a book review.

Hardcover ISBN: 9798822963108

Paperback ISBN: 9798822963115

This book is dedicated to my wife Virginia who has patiently supported me throughout the years in various endeavors I have engaged in, even when the outcomes seemed unlikely. And to the Lord Jesus Christ for providing me not only the inspiration and abilities to complete this work, but also the friends and families who gave their support for this project.

Contents

Introduction: Sources xi

Prologue: The Genesis of El Rio xiii

Chapter One: The Early Days 1

Chapter Two: The Crossroads at Vineyard and Ventura Boulevard   9

Chapter Three: El Rio Developments 35

Chapter Four: Portraits El Rio Pioneers 49

Epilogue. 57

INTRODUCTION

SOURCES

In presenting this portrayal of the development of El Rio, it's always possible while reviewing history that incorrect perspectives can be concluded. This could be based on limited information and conclusions that others have come to in their research. It's understood that some misunderstandings can change when new information is obtained. Please be assured that I've made every effort to provide accurate, truthful, and confirmed conclusions based on the information available to me. Sources for which I am most grateful are referenced in developing this history are as follows:

Thompson and West History of Ventura County 1883, California National Register of Historic listings in Ventura County, *A Memorial and Biographical History of the Counties of Santa Barbara, San Luis Obispo, and Ventura, California* by Mrs. Yda Addis Storke 1891, *History of Ventura County* by Sol Sheridan 1926, *History of the Jews in Ventura County* by Diane Mautner, *A Tower in the Valley* by Catherine Mervyn 1989, *Legendary Locals of Oxnard* by Jeffrey Wayne Maulhardt 2013, and *The Riverpark Specific Plan: Historic Resources Report and the Ventura County Genealogical Society*, and Olga Nares.

Information herein was taken from articles and other historical sources. These articles were written in 1923, 1925, 1929, 1949, 1966, 1967, 1973, 1979, 1980, 1982, 1987, 1989, 1991, 1992, 1994, 2000, and 2002. They recount various historic facts about New Jerusalem/El Rio, which covers the history and families and the future of this little slice of the Promised Land.

However these articles were done piecemeal over those years, and some duplicate the same information such as the founding of El Rio. The following is my effort to bring together this information to provide a single historical and chronological source so the reader can have a fact-based history of the township and the citizens that birthed so many positive developments in the young county of Ventura in the Santa Clara Valley. More of this information is also covered under chapter two footnotes.

Prologue

THE GENESIS OF EL RIO

All births involve an umbilical cord. This review attempts clarification to the birth and history of the township named New Jerusalem/El Rio. This covers the Chumash, Mexican, Jewish, and Irish legacy of El Rio. In tracing El Rio's DNA, the following facts are submitted.

Chapter One

THE EARLY DAYS

Chumash

CALIFORNIA INDIANS GROUP PHOTO
Image

The history of California can be divided into four periods with the Native American period about ten thousand years ago until 1542.

Before there was any California or even a United States for that matter, Native American Indian populations had lived throughout the country. These populations were compromised by various tribes who shared and differed in their cultural aspects but were the original inhabitants of our nation.

In El Rio's case, the Chumash were the original inhabitants who had occupied the islands and areas all along the California coast and inland (such as the Saticoy) areas. They were a peaceful people who had been there for thousands of years before the Spanish discovered California. These were the people encountered by Juan Rodriguez Cabrillo on Tuesday, October 10, 1542 (Yda Addis Storke).

Santa Barbara/Ventura County Chumash

It must be remembered that before Santa Barbara and Ventura County were founded, these areas were actually Chumash tribal areas. Therefore we have reached back to what had been determined in the 1999 final report called *Cultural Affiliation and Lineal Descents of Chumash Peoples in the Channel Islands and Santa Monica Mountains* for our information.

Although there are many other Chumash descendants throughout the county and state, this portion of that history of the genesis of El Rio will focus on the Chumash who populated the area that would become El Rio. The periods are between 1756 and 1907, which identify these descendants as Muwu and Lisiqishi lineages. If the reader wishes more details than provided here, it is recommended that the *Cultural Affiliation and Lineal Descent of Chumash Peoples in the Channel Islands and Santa Monica Mountains* be reviewed.

El Rio Chumash

Beginning with Maria Agapita Supilmehuu, 1733–1825, the accompanying flow charts, trace those descendants all the way through 1907. Her son Manual Juan Liguinaihichu, born 1789, was most likely a Lisiqishi Chief as only chiefs were allowed to have two wives, and his were Maria Julia Sajutienahuan and Maria Clemencia Putalmenahuan.

Manuel had three children, one of which was Valentin de Jesus Guilaliachet, born in 1807. Valentin had a daughter Policarpa born in 1836. Coleta de Jesus Alulupienahuanborn, born in 1866, had three grandchildren, and her son Harmeneglldo was born in 1824. He appears to have been married to Valentin's daughter Policarpa.

She had a son named Jose Juan de Jusus. (later known as Juan Miller). Jose's baptismal records list his father as Harmeneglldo, but his actual father was an American German rancher named Miller. Jose (Juan de Jesus) Miller later married Maria Alaya and lived in El Rio. They had at least three children. These descendants at the end of the flow charts are identified as follows:

Juan Angel Miller, 1899–1972; this writer's grandfather Marcos Antonio Miller, 1901–1933; and Martha Miller, 1907–1987. Many of these families' descendants still live in the El Rio and Oxnard communities.

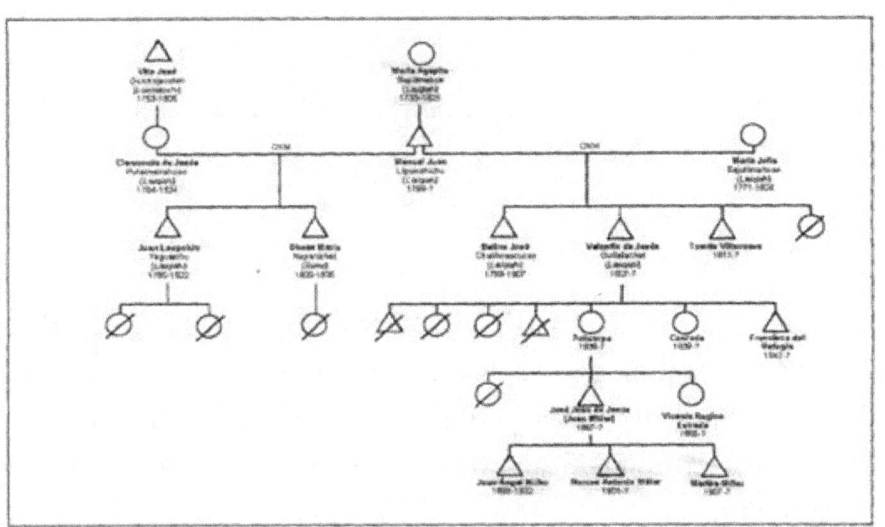

Figure 11.8 *Lisiaishi* Lineage 1: Descendants of Maria Agapita Supilimehue

1769–1821: The Ranchos

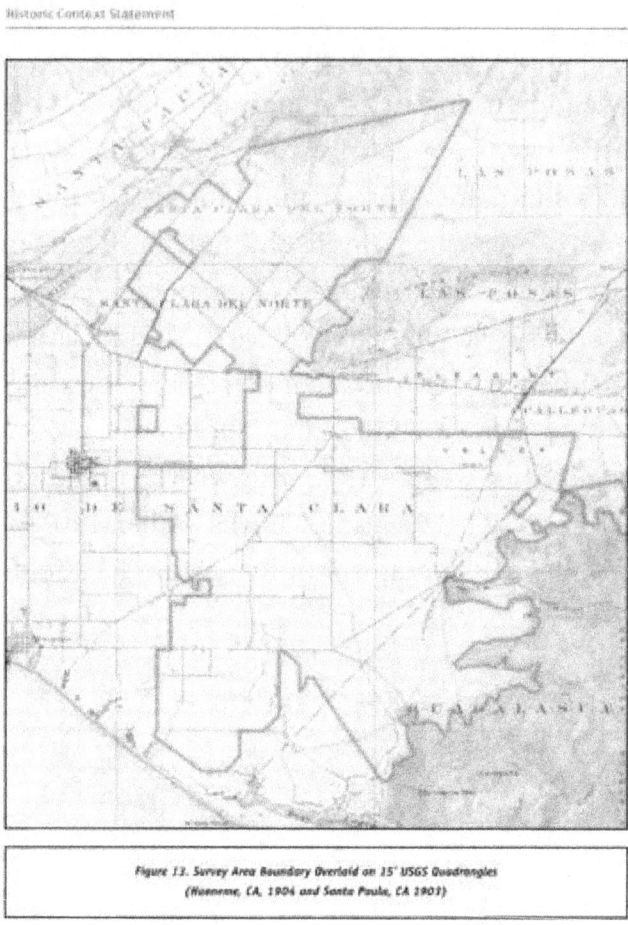

Figure 13. Survey Area Boundary Overlaid on 15' USGS Quadrangles (Hueneme, CA, 1904 and Santa Paula, CA 1903)

Subsequent to the Chumash in California, there followed the European exploration period that existed from 1542 to 1769, then followed the Spanish colonial period from 1769 to 1821, the Mexican period from 1821 to 1848, and the United States period from 1848 to the present.

During the Spanish colonial period, land grants were given to Spanish soldiers of the Santa Barbara presidio or garrison. One of these land grants was called Rancho Santa Clara Del Norte, and on May 6, 1837, it was granted to Juan M. Sanchez (1791–1873), a former Santa Barbara Presidio soldier (Wikipedia).

By 1864 most of the land grants had been sold, and between 1866–1868 they were subdivided into smaller parcels for sale as farmlands and ranches. Hence streets in El Rio were named after sixteenth-century conquistadores such as Cortez, Balboa, Alvarado, and Corsicana.

An article written in July 1929 by E. M. Sheridan states that Vineyard Avenue got its name from the Dominguez vineyard, which was on the highway a half a mile from El Rio toward Saticoy. Dominguez's vineyard was where much wine and brandy were made in the 1870s and was quite famous. The ranch house was great for the young folks because of the dances that were held there regularly on Saturday nights. The young folks from around the county would gather there at these dances in great numbers and dance from sundown to sunup. A 1923 article states that Ventura Boulevard was also El Camino Real.

1868–1869: The Campbellites/The Disciples of Christ

A 1923 article states that in 1868–1869 a Campbellite preacher brought several families of the Disciples of Christ to the area to settle there. The section was a crossroads at the border between two big ranches, Rancho Santa Clara del Norte, which would become El Rio, and El Rio o La Colonia, which would later become Oxnard. These ranches came together and sometimes overlapped in the area that is now Vineyard Avenue and Oxnard Boulevard. The Campbellites built a little framed church and stayed for a time but gradually drifted away.

1872–1873: The New County of Ventura

The Agony Over, and Everything Lovely !

FRIDAY NIGHT, March 22.

We stop the press to announce that Governor Booth has just signed the bill creating the new county of Ventura, and it is now a law.

So the long suspense is over, and on the First day of January, 1873, Ventura will take its place in the constellation of Counties of California.

At this point it is important to remember that Santa Barbara extended all the way to the Los Angeles County line. Legislation separating Santa Barbara and creating Ventura County was passed by the senate on March 22, 1872, taking effect January 1, 1873. In his *History of Ventura County 1883*, Myron Angel describes the creation of Ventura County in full detail.

Within a short time (1875) another event would occur that would have a permanent and everlasting impact on the county of Ventura.

The agricultural and favorable potential of the area caused many people to start looking toward what was once called the Colony by the River as a place to stake their futures on.

A February 7, 1923, article states that the crossroads at Vineyard Avenue and Ventura Boulevard were also known by other names such as Death Corner due to the volume of fatal accidents there. It was considered the most dangerous intersection on the state highway. It was also called Centreville. It also states that El Rio had one brick building and a number of shacks. On one corner was a haunted garage whose operator, Carl Stannard, was murdered by an Alfred Ellis. There were seven saloons going full blast all the time. Trouble was settled with bare fists.

There were three shootings, and a man named McCoy killed his wife. Also mentioned are the bones of five skeletons being found in El Rio.

The Sheridan article stated that it was quite a pretentious place with good schools, churches, a number of homes, and the post office where Simon Cohn was postmaster.

A 1949 article recounts the memories of Mrs. Cohn, the widow of Simon Cohn who died in 1936. It recounts the Biblical abundance of cattle, fruit, milk, and honey in New Jerusalem.

She also mentions the impacts the 1906 San Francisco earthquake and collapse of the St. Frances dam in 1928, which took more than four hundred lives, had on El Rio.

She describes the harsh conditions that Mexican farm women had to endure. She says they worked as slaves, cooking for their large families and for the hired men. They came from the old country and helped their husbands build new homes. They did everything.

1875: The Father of New Jerusalem/El Rio Simon Cohn

Simon Cohn was a Jewish German immigrant who settled in El Rio in 1875, two years after Ventura County was created. This photo is of Cohn's store in 1936. Further details will be provided in chapter four.

Chapter Two

THE CROSSROADS AT VINEYARD AND VENTURA BOULEVARD FOOTNOTES #1 1876–1889

These seventeen pages describe how life was in New Jerusalem in those times. Biographical histories and news articles were written between 1876 and 1889. News publications such as the *Signal*, *Free Press*, and *Vidette* authored articles that described life in New Jerusalem as well as calling it the unholy land. The information is valuable as it covers many subjects such as the Jewish history of El Rio.

They explain the development of the post office and that El Rio was also called Centreville, the Crossroads, and the Colonia. Other facts describe Santa Clara chapel and many other subjects and issues. Who compiled this information is not known and was discovered during my research at the Ventura County Historical Museum. These facts merit their own chapter. This information is amazing.

New Jerusalem: The Unholy Land Footnotes

1. *The Ventura Signal*, April 29, 1876
2. *The Ventura Signal*, September 15, 1877
3. *The Ventura Free Press*, July 20, 1887
4. *The Ventura Free Press*, December 1, 1877
5. *The Ventura Free Press*, December 18, 1875
6. *The Ventura Free Press*, May 28, 1886
7. *The Ventura Free Press*, March 3, 1877
8. *The Ventura Signal*, March 23, 1878
9. *The Ventura Signal*, February 24, 1883
10. *The Ventura Free Press*, September 29, 1883
11. *The Ventura Signal*, January 27, 1883
12. *The Ventura Signal*, August 23, 1884
13. *The Ventura Signal*, April 19, 1884
14. *The Ventura Signal*, March 15, 1884
15. *The Ventura Free Press*, March 29, 1884
16. *The Ventura Free Press*, November 6, 1885
17. *The Ventura Signal*, September 6, 1884
18. *The Ventura Free Press*, October 2, 1885
19. *The Ventura Free Press*, October 9, 1885

20. *The Ventura Vidette*, August 3, 1889
21. *The Ventura Free Press*, January 16, 1889
22. *The Ventura Vidette*, June 15, 1889
23. *The Ventura Free Press*, December 31, 1886
24. *The Ventura Free Press*, January 16, 1889

New Jerusalem: The Unholy Land

Whiskey is a good thing in its place. There is nothing like it for preserving a man when he is dead. —Guthrie

In the beginning they called it Centreville, an appropriate name when one considers that it was the contemporary geographical center of things. As the crow flies, it was almost equidistant between San Buenaventura and Hueneme, give or take a few flaps of the wings, and Saticoy to the northeast and Springville to the southeast were approximately equal flying time—if one permitted the crow a slight pause at Parson Wood's corn patch or a detour to the vineyards of Señors Sanchez and Dominquez on Rancho Santa Clara del Norte.

If Centreville was anything more than a name for the principal crossroads of the county, the contemporary newspaper, the *Ventura Signal*, failed to record what was there. In all probability the winery of Roberto Dominquez and an old adobe or two acting as a primitive emergency holding point for stagecoaches when the Santa Clara River Was at flood stage would cover the full development of Centreville.

Five years later it was called New Jerusalem, a name to be reckoned with by every sheriff and peace officer for years to come. As a place name on the maps of the county, New Jerusalem first appeared in 1875. The manner of its christening was described in 1876 (although how accurately might be open to argument) by a traveling correspondent for one of the Santa Barbara newspapers. "We halt at New Jerusalem, a little, trading station—so called because two Jews opened a trading post at this point, and like their forefathers in Jerusalem of old, they cheated each other, quarreled, and divided their goods, and still continue to quarrel."

If the reader suspects a bit of anti-Semitism in the above quoted news item, he is probably correct. By 1877 there was talk of establishing a post office at New Jerusalem, a name that appears to have been repugnant to at least one gentile in the village. "There is considerable talk of changing the name of our town. Let it be done by all means before we get a Post-office. The name 'Centreville' and 'Colonia' have been suggested. Let others be named, have a meeting called at Daly & Rogers' Hall and all invited to attend."

If the meeting was ever held and a vote to change the name approved, it was never cleared with Simon Cohn, the town burgomaster. It was not until five years later, on July 26, 1882, that the post office was finally established; its name was New Jerusalem, and the first postmaster was Simon Cohn. On February 5, 1895, the name of the office was shortened to Jerusalem and shortly thereafter to El Rio.

But the gentiles died hard. *The Ventura Free Press* on July 6, 1887, carried a large subdivision advertisement for Taylor & Jepson's new townsite south of the river headed: "Jerusalem to the Front." By July 19, enough pressure had been brought to bear on the developers that the advertisement was changed to: "Taylor & Jepson's New Town Site of Colonia…on the Proposed Branch of the S. P. R. R. to Hueneme."

The following day the *Free Press* cleared up any lingering doubts in respect to the location of Colonia with two short news items:

"Colonia and New Jerusalem are one and the same place, and there's lots of money in it for investors."

"New Jerusalem has had its name changed to Colonia."

For ninety days Colonia and its get-rich-quick developers crowded the *Free Press* with brief news items of their new subdivision, the grand finale of which was a lottery for town lots in the new metropolis. With the drawing out of the way in mid-November, Colonia vanished from the newspaper scene forever. Obviously Taylor & Jepson had not cleared the scheme with Simon Cohn.

When it was not called Centreville, New Jerusalem, Jerusalem, Colonia, or El Rio, it was frequently referred to as the Crossroads, a name that could not have been more appropriate. Here was the principal intersection for Ventura County traffic well into the twentieth century, with the Conejo stage road (later Highway 101) leading from San Buenaventura to Los Angeles and Vineyard Avenue from Hueneme (and later Oxnard) to Rancho Santa Clara del Norte and the upper Santa Clara Valley east of Saticoy. Simon Cohn would live to see those crossroads manufacture more scrap steel than any other place in Ventura County—before some genius invented the boulevard stop. Until the day the historic old building was pushed out by the bulldozers to make way for the modern freeway interchange, Simon Cohn's general store bore the scars of uncountable wrecks that had slithered and slammed into his heavy-duty front porch. The automobile never won an encounter with Simon Cohn's New Jerusalem, but like Taylor & Jepson, it tried.

The Santa Barbara correspondent's explanation of the naming of New Jerusalem gave no clue with respect to the identity of the two Jews who had established the trading post at the Crossroads. However, the *Ventura Signal* on October 30, 1875, published a legal notice of the dissolution of the partnership of Simon Cohn and Samuel Herbst "by mutual consent." They may have quarreled, and they undoubtedly divided their goods, but if there was any cheating done, it was not on the part of Simon Cohn. Simon would live and manage his general store at the Crossroads until his death on November 16, 1936. No man stays in business in one location for sixty-one years, earns the love and respect of his fellow man, becomes a living legend in his own time, and accomplishes the feat by cheating.

Not that there wasn't some cheating in evidence in the town. Two years after Cohn & Herbst dissolved their partnership, the *Ventura Free Press* ran the following news item: "Last Saturday night, while Mr. Simon Cohn of New Jerusalem, was absent at a social party, somebody broke into his store and carried off about $500 worth of clothing, boots and shoes, etc. Mr. Cohn procured the arrest of a neighbor on a charge of burglary, but there was not the slightest evidence against the man, and the prosecution entered a nolle prosequi…"

At 1877 prices, five hundred dollars' worth of merchandise would have established a fair-sized trading post, and Simon Cohn knew it. Only another merchant in the area could have used that amount of goods, and Simon knew that too. But as the news account intimated, knowing and proving were two different things.

As early as the Christmas season of 1875, Simon Cohn realized he had settled in a region that was nearly the equal of any in the legendary Wild West for gunplay, rowdiness, and drunkenness.

> Between 9 and 10 o'clock Thursday night last, Mr. Simon Cohn informs us, an attempt was made to murder him in his store and to set fire to the building. Mr. Cohn lives in a little town on the La Colonia ranch, which goes by the euphonious name of New Jerusalem. and the man—one W.
>
> H. Wilson—who has until recently been in the employe of Wm. Evans, near Saticoy, seemed actuated by a desire to not only carry out the prophecy, by not, leaving one stone upon another, but also to exterminate the Israelites of this New Jerusalem, Mr.

Cohn informs us that the individual came to his store and asked to be admitted (after the place had closed for the night) and upon being questioned as to what he wanted made no reply. Mr. Cohn refused him entrance at that hour, and he then fired two shots at him with a double-barreled shot gun, but fortunately neither took effect. Mr. Cohn informs us that after the shots were fired the man declared that if he did not give him some powder he would set the house on fire and murder him. Mr. Cohn procured the assistance of Chas. Wilson, Esq., and succeeded in capturing the murderously inclined individual, whom they securely tied and brought to this place yesterday. Mr. Cohn says that the man seemed about half drunk.

In the interests of accuracy it should be noted that Simon Cohn did not live on La Colonia, but rather on Rancho Santa Clara del Norte, the Conejo stage road being the dividing line between the two ranchos. That part of New Valley had the vineyards of Roberto Dominquez within a mile of New Jerusalem and the farms of Tom Williams and Mr. Owens nearby.

The improvements in "the finest location for a city in the Santa Clara Valley" were listed in 1877 by the *Free Press*. "The hotel at New Jerusalem is nearly completed. Of the six buildings in the place, two are blacksmith shops and three keep 'a drap o' the craythur' for sale. We hear that another bar is soon to be started there."

A *drap o' the craythur* may need defining for those Texans of non-Irish ancestry.

Brewer's 1898 edition of *Dictionary of Phrase and Fable* states that a drop of the crathur "in Ireland means a drink of whiskey or 'creature comfort.'" Webster defines *creatures* as being a humorous reference to whiskey. Another source states that in Old Irish dialect, *crathur* (or *craythur*) means creature, which in turn can be defined as the devil himself. It can be assumed with absolute assurance that in 1877, "a drap o' the craythur" by any definition was a reasonable facsimile of a liquid approaching 100 proof.

Between 1877 and early 1883, very little appeared in the Ventura newspapers respecting the misbehavior of the citizens south of the Santa Clara River. A robbery or two, an arrest for disturbing the peace, and a couple of suspected arson cases being the sum total of complaints published. Possibly the newspapers of San Buenaventura became tired of printing news of the customary brawlings in that burg, but it was also possible that Father Farrelly and the first Catholic church south of the river had a sobering influence thereon. The account of the opening of the little parish station conveys in splendid style the cosmopolitan nature of Ranchos La Colonia and Santa Clara del Norte and their little trading center of New Jerusalem:

> On last Sunday, the 17th of March, the new Catholic Church at New Jerusalem was formally opened. Father Gelss sang the Mass and preached a sermon in German. After the ceremonies, Father Farrelly, pastor at this place, addressed the large congregation in English and Spanish. There were a large number of people of all classes and denominations present. It being St. Patrick's Day, our Irish fellow-citizens turned out en masse, displaying the national emblem, the shamrock. The church will be dedicated as soon as the debts are all paid, which it is hoped will be very soon. The church is a neat frame building 26 × 50 feet, with an entry way in front, and was built at a cost of $1500, is in a rich section of the country, and we doubt not the church will be well sustained and soon paid for.

It is purely conjectural on the part of the writer, but with the Irish turning out en masse wearing the shamrock on St. Patrick's Day, the omission of any mention of "a drap o' the crathur" must be considered an oversight on the part of the reporter.

The New Jerusalem Catholic Church was not officially dedicated until November 1883. Two weeks later the *Signal* announced that

$1700 had been raised to provide the church with a resident priest, indicating that some difficulty may have been encountered during the intervening five years in financing a pastor on a permanent basis.

Never was any locale more in need of spiritual assistance. Earlier in the year, a traveling correspondent had written of the place:

> New Jerusalem—The livest embryo city in Ventura County is wicked and glories in its iniquities. We like the place, in fact we were madly in love with it, but we did not stay there very long. Accustomed to Sunday somnolence in the metropolis, New Jerusalem was a little too lively for us. It is glorious to shoot dogs which have taken refuge under the heels of a six-horse team, but when the sport is participated in by twenty or thirty howling dervishes who have become so wrought up with religious frenzy—or something worse—as not to be able to distinguish the dog from the horses, the sport becomes too exhilirating for us. New Jerusalem is a nice place, but we did not like the climate, and when a man with a loaded shot-gun inquired what our business was, we went away from there. We had some business to attend to, but it was not in the nature of blowing into the muzzle of a gun to see what kind of shot it is loaded with.

At the same time that the above news item appeared in the *Signal*, the *Thompson & West History of Ventura And Santa Barbara Counties* was being distributed to subscribers. It is interesting to compare the latter's description of New Jerusalem with the contemporary news account:

> New Jerusalem is a promising little village on the Santa. Clara del Norte Rancho, about eight miles east of San Buenaventura, and near the east bank of the Santa Clara River where the county road to Los Angeles crosses that stream. It Is located the midst of a rich farming district with good schools, stores, and shops, and a very fine Catholic Church.

Technically speaking there can be no quarrel with the accuracy of the *Thompson & West* statement, although there might be some argument over the quality of the stores and shops since at least four of them were saloons. And the statement that New Jerusalem was "a promising little village" could have been better defined in respect to precisely what it was "promising." The truth of the matter was that it was promising to become the toughest little town south of Bodie and west of Dodge City.

Later in the year, one Jose Jimenez and a companion came riding into town in a buggy, blazing away with their revolvers in the best Wild West tradition. "A bullet struck the ground in the yard of Mr. McManus, close to where his children were playing. That gentleman rode into town and procured the fellow's arrest. He pleaded guilty and Judge Hamer thought 50 days behind bars would be about the proper dose. Correct."

The same year Simon Cohn had officiated on a coroner's jury deliberating the accidental shooting of a young girl by her brother with an "unloaded gun." The unofficial mayor of New Jerusalem expressed in no uncertain terms the growing feelings of the more serious minded of the county on the problem of firearms and their use: "We … wish in the most earnest manner to express our censure of the carelessness displayed in handling firearms without knowing whether the same are loaded or not."

The point may seem insignificant in view of the fact that every gun-toter in the area knew very well that his gun was loaded and ready for legitimate use, but what constituted legitimate use was not always well defined.

The following year J. D. McCoy shot his wife in the leg in self-defense after Mrs. McCoy had attacked him with a hatchet. *The Signal* noted that Madam McCoy was a second wife and was said to possess much temper. The authorities considered this a legitimate use for a gun, although whether on the grounds of Mrs. McCoy's temper, remarriage, or the hatchet she attempted to bury in her husband's chest (with some success) was not specified.

The Ventura Free Press reported on August 22, 1884, that "Frank Ayala was shot Saturday night by young Romero at New Jerusalem. Romero was arrested and brought to town and in default of $1000 bond now languishes in jail…"

The Ventura Signal on the following day gave a much more detailed account of the affair, one which could well have been taken from the script of any television "Western":

> At New Jerusalem Friday night, in Carrillo & Edwards' saloon, three men, Octaviano Romero, Frank Ayala, and a young man by the name of Kalisher were shaking dice for money. Romero was losing and accused Ayala of unfair play. He lost his pile and went out, soon returning with twenty dollars and resuming play. He bad lost all this but fifty cents, which was in the pot, and lost that when the dice were turned. Instead of submitting, however, to the loss he grabbed the money from the table, jumped up from his chair, drew his revolver, denounced Ayala, and fired almost all at one and the same time. Ayala was turned sideways toward him, and the ball from Romero's pistol struck him close up under the right arm, ploughing its way through the flesh near the surface. He attempted to fire again, but was prevented by Edwards, one of the proprietors of the house.
>
> He was arrested, brought to town and caged…

This was obviously considered an illegitimate use of firearms under the standards of the day, unless Ayala had, indeed, been cheating.

The next month a man named Kohr shot his wife after buying

a cheap gun (there was really no point in purchasing an expensive weapon for such a purpose) and then committed suicide. *The Free Press* made the rather apparent observation that the husband had a bad disposition.

Both newspapers of San Buenaventura were strongly of the opinion that the shootings and lawlessness south of the river could all be blamed on liquor and an overabundance of saloons in New Jerusalem. The fourth estate was undoubtedly correct up to a point. The only other trading centers were Hueneme and Springville, where T. R. Bard and Parson Wood, respectively, kept a much tighter rein on the behavior patterns of the citizens. But with a huge, landed area inhabited by a diverse cosmopolitan population, it was almost preordained that some place should act as a center for frolicking and frivolity. New Jerusalem was it.

The year 1884 was a banner one for the Crossroads, with the *Signal* noting in its issue of January 5 that the "afternoon matinee was liberally interspersed with whiskey and free fights.

Later in the evening the performers adjourned to Dominquez winery, where one poor devil was slashed to mincemeat, and the rest were injured more or less."

The same issue noted an even more interesting item with the announcement that "the post office and beer have dissolved partnership. The post office will hereafter be kept at Walbridge's and the beer at Cohn's." The item is of importance since few people associate Simon Cohn with the saloon or liquor business. There is sufficient evidence to indicate, however, that he severed all connections therefrom in November 1885, for good and sufficient reasons.

But in 1884 things were different. Early in the year, Mr. Cohn went to Los Angeles, presumably on a short business trip, only to be detained there by the great floods of that year. In his absence his brother, Leopold, "remodeled" the saloon by what the *Signal* called the Lightening Process. He frescoed the ceiling, veneered the wainscoting, and plastered dados from top to bottom. In a scene reminiscent of a Santa Barbara Channel oil well blow out, "a slip of the bung and all was over—that is the beer was all over. Leopold, alias Tadpole, received a full benefit in the face."

The floods of 1884 had a sobering influence on New Jerusalem, for a short time at least.

The rains commenced on January 26 and continued for eleven days without letup. San Buenaventura, normally one of the lightest rainfall points in the county, received 11.29 inches, with far higher readings recorded in the interior regions. All news from New Jerusalem concerning "a drap o' the craythur" was replaced by reports of heroic rescues from the flooding Santa Clara River. Overturned stagecoaches, lost mail bags retrieved by daredevil Californians on horseback, and an occasional drowning became the order of the day. No one in his right mind ever attempted the crossing at New Jerusalem during high water, but the place was just far enough down river from the Saticoy ford for the convenient rescue of those who had been unsuccessful upriver.

One week later the storm hit again on a water-soaked land, and although the rainfall was not so great, the flood far exceeded that of the earlier storm. Again New Jerusalem was the center of rescue operations for those foolish enough to attempt the Saticoy ford.

Jupiter Pluvius retired for twelve days and then unloosed a third major storm between March 3 and March 9. By that time the Ventura rain gauges measured twenty-eight inches, all but four of which had fallen after January 26. At New Jerusalem, as in the rest of the county, the flood took precedence, even over a mug of beer:

> More rain, more rest.
>
> The river still keeps up so that it is rather dangerous crossing yet. One man, a Spaniard from Santa Barbara was drowned Tuesday while crossing on horseback, his horse swam out. Diligent search has been made for his body but it has not been recovered...
>
> Those inhabitants near the river moved twice during the latest high water; the house occupied by Vasquez and his family has been moved farther away from the river which is within a few yards of place her it stood...

It would be late June 1884 before the *Free Press* published the last news of a heavy storm delaying stagecoaches and rolling rocks in the creeks and river. By that time over thirty-six inches of rain had fallen in Ventura, thirty-two of which fell after January 26.

Those citizens caught on the south side of the river during the flood siege had but one place to stay—New Jerusalem. Among the unfortunates was the Reverend Mr. Wenck, preacher at the Santa Paula Methodist Church. It was pure coincidence that little news of whiskey shenanigans appeared in the newspapers during the Reverend Wenck's sojourn in the unholy land. However, that worthy was more than willing to risk life and limb to get out of the place:

> The Rev. Mr. Wenck, of Santa Paula, was detained in this vicinity for three weeks and attempted an escape Tuesday, but after receiving a thorough ducking in the river, he concluded to come back and see how far he had got. We heard this morning, however, that he attempted it again and made a better success of it. His buggy sustained some damage.

There may have been more than met the eye in the above news item. The editor of the *Free Press* at the time was the Reverend Dr.

Stephen Bowers, himself a Methodist. Eighteen months later upon the marriage of Reverend Wenck, Bowers's *Free Press* reported: "We learn that Miss Dull, formerly of Santa Paula, has married Rev. W. F. Wenck. He has done well, if we can't say quite so much for her."

Whatever inspired that comment from a fellow man of the cloth has been lost to history, but the enforced sojourn of the Reverend Wenck in New Jerusalem during the 1884 floods did nothing to abate or reform the free-for-all carousing in that tour. With the river and weather back to some semblance of normalcy, New Jerusalem could look forward to a busy summer. *The Free Press* commented on June 6 that "Sunday was a fair specimen of what we may expect all summer, our little burg was full from morning until midnight, the folks also were full."

Complaints of the behavior of New Jerusalem's customers had reached such proportions by June 1884, that the Ventura County Board of Supervisors took feeble cognizance of the problem and appointed a special deputy sheriff to police the town—on Sundays. *The Signal* correspondent noted that this gave some assurance of quiet times and peaceful Sundays as in other civilized cities, while the *Free Press* expressed concern lest the citizens of that place would next request that the county seat be moved south of the river.

The only effect that a deputy sheriff appears to have had on New Jerusalem was to drive the lawless element out into the suburbs for their after drinking pleasures. "Sunday was a lively day. It is very evident that some of the 'bloods' have a little respect for our holy city, for they go out in the suburbs to fight."

The following years were a repetition of 1884, with only the details varying enough to prevent monotonous repetition. More thievery was noted, resulting in a demand in 1885 for the formation of a vigilante society. That year also saw the reestablishment of the copartnership of post office and beer when Simon Cohn again became postmaster of New Jerusalem. The reunion resulted in a mild exchange of letters in the *Free Press*, which was destined to cause little commotion but which resulted in a fine contemporary description of the town for the future historian:

> Editor Free Press: Will you be so kind as to insert these few lines in your valuable paper. In passing the other day through a small town about eight miles south of Ventura, called New Jerusalem, I was astonished at the number of saloons existing in the place. The entire town is composed of twelve buildings occupied as follows: Five saloons, one of them closed; three blacksmith shops, two of them closed; two private residences, closed; and a church. I was informed that the postmaster of that place keeps in the same building, and entering through the same door, postoffice, general merchandise, saloon, and billard table. I would like to know if the law allows a postmaster so many incentives to immorality.
>
> Can you inform me, Mr. Editor?

The letter was signed "Traveler" and brought forth a vigorous denial of the charges from an unidentified resident of New Jerusalem:

> Your 'Traveler' of last week was either misinformed concerning our little city or had got afoul of some crooked whiskey. The place is bad enough at best without any exaggeration. We have more than two private residences and there is no liquor or billiard table in the postoffice building. In fact, to put it in mild language, it is a lie from beginning to end.

The reader is at liberty to choose which version is the more accurate, although a certain degree of equivocation seems noticeable in the second letter. They are quoted here for a more important reason. Simon Cohn had become postmaster at the beginning of the year, and if he still held that position in October, the first letter quoted above is the last reference found by this writer to Mr. Cohn being in the liquor business. On November 8, 1885, he was married to Miss Minnie Cohn (no relation), and Mrs. Cohn is known to have detested the very word *saloon*. None of their eight children who are still living ever knew that their father had, in the early days before his marriage, been in the liquor dispensing business. It is pure conjecture on the writer's part, but it seems apparent that Simon Cohn faced a choice of getting out of the liquor business once and for all or remaining a bachelor.

Life at the Crossroads continued on its merry ways, with only the more serious brawls rating newspaper space anymore. When one Miguel Arrelanes skewered the Chinese cook on the Ayers threshing machine outfit with a pitchfork, the *Free Press* thought it had enough news value to report the incident in detail. By 1889 a fight in New Jerusalem was no longer news, but when a Sunday passed without a fight, the *Ventura Vidette* felt obligated to report such a novelty: "A reporter today asked a resident of New Jerusalem the stereotyped question, what's the news? 'Nothing,' said he, 'except we had no fights out our way Sunday.' The law and order element of New Jerusalem is to be congratulated."

Early in 1889 the Ventura County Board of Supervisors felt the situation across the river to be of enough importance to warrant a special jail at New Jerusalem. Supervisor Dudley was appointed a committee of one "to superintend the construction of a calaboose at New Jerusalem, cost not to exceed $100."[21] But bureaucracy moved as slowly in 1889 as it does today, or possibly Supervisor Dudley found $100 an insufficient fund to construct a jail sturdy enough to withstand the Colonia lawless, for prisoners were still being brought to San Buenaventura in June.

The Ventura Vidette on June 15, 1889, reported that a tramp named Fred Jones "now pines in the Hotel Rodriquez" in Ventura for molesting the property of saloon keeper Geisler in New Jerusalem. Jones had been sleeping outside the saloon and rolling his blankets in the morning and leaving them there, much to the annoyance of Geisler. The saloon keeper finally picked them up and ordered Jones to move on, whereupon the tramp ordered that his blanket roll be restored to their original position, with the ultimatum that if they were not, he would heave a rock through the saloon window upon the count of three.

"One, two, three."

Crash!

"Justice Cook arrested Jones and deputized Mr. Rice to bring the curve pitcher to town."

The Vidette pointed out on July 6 that a jail in New Jerusalem would be a large savings to the taxpayers of the county:

> A reporter was yesterday informed that if transportation fees throughout the year average monthly what they have for the last few months, $65 a month will be the figure—$780 a year for bringing prisoners from New Jerusalem to the jail here. Now a small jail could be built at New Jerusalem for at most $150. The ground would cost nothing. Here then is a savings of more than $600 the first year to the taxpayers. Then there is another and greater advantage in having a jail at New Jerusalem. As it is now, when prisoners have to be brought to this place, officers are delicate about arresting all offenders, owing to the large expense attached thereto. So that a jail at New Jerusalem would not only be a matter of economy, but, as well, of better protection to the law-abiding citizens of San Pedro Township. It is hoped the Board will consider this matter their next meeting.

There may have been reasons other than economy why officers were "delicate about arresting all offenders" at New Jerusalem, but the point is minor.

The lumber for the new jail arrived late in July, and it had come none too soon. The July 27 issue of the *Vidette* reported that construction of the town's sixth saloon was already under way.

Much of the information concerning New Jerusalem between 1883 and 1890 was published in the *Ventura Free Press*, and later the *Vidette*, when those newspapers were being edited by Dr. Stephen Bowers, a Methodist minister. It is significant that during the period between August 1887 and June 1889, when the *Free Press* was under different ownership, that very little was published about New Jerusalem. And while the Crossroads was undoubtedly the roaringest little town in the county, one finds it difficult to sympathize with Bowers and his eternal moralizing after reading the description of New Jerusalem he published in a special eight-page edition of the *Free Press* that was intended for eastern circulation to entice immigrants into the county:

> New Jerusalem—Is situated on the east bank of the Santa Clara River, seven miles east of the county seat. The surrounding country is exceedingly inviting and very productive. The town is well located. It has two stores, a hotel, restaurant, two blacksmith shops a church, postoffice and a schoolhouse adjacent.

Bowers was either guilty of gross exaggeration in his news accounts of New Jerusalem behavior on the one hand or rank deceit on the other when he threw out that bait for the benefit of the potential midwest immigrant. No self-respecting farmer in the Bible Belt would have brought his family within a country mile of the place after reading the Ventura newspaper accounts of the Sabbath shenanigans in New Jerusalem. But if all he knew was what Bowers had written in that special edition, the lure of a country "exceedingly inviting and very productive" would have been like dangling a night crawler in front of a bass.

The feelings of the population in general in respect to New Jerusalem were probably best expressed by a letter writer during one of the periodic attempts to finance a bridge across the Santa Clara River: "If people will go to or trough Jerusalem they ought to wade."[24]

Through it all the town's first citizen, Simon Cohn, sat on a bread box on the massive front porch of his general store watching the world go by and being a friend of man. Simon had arrived at the Crossroads just in time to see the last of the Coast Line stagecoaches using the old Conejo stage road before they were rerouted to the Santa Clara Valley. He had watched Roberto Dominquez tramp out the Santa Clara del Norte grapes into wine by the old barefoot process and had a ringside seat to watch the results of the overconsumption of that product.

When Henry T. Oxnard started construction of the massive sugar factory on the barren plains between New Jerusalem and Hueneme in 1897, Simon Cohn had watched his neighbors pick up their belongings, homes, saloons, and business houses and move body and soul to start the city that, by all the rules of logic, should have been located at El Rio.

It was probably with mixed emotions that he watched them go—relief that the tough element that had given New Jerusalem its unsavory reputation would henceforth make Oxnard the Sodom and Gomorrah of Ventura County, but sadness because the Crossroads had been forsaken as the location for the future metropolis south of the river.

If any temptation presented itself to follow the crowd, he pushed it aside. Simon Cohn would remain with his store at New Jerusalem, even though the gentiles had finally prevailed upon the post office department to change the name to El Rio. Simon went along with the change to the extent of painting the new name on the front of his general store, but New Jerusalem still remained through the years on the Vineyard Avenue side of the first brick building to be built south of the Santa Clara River (1881).

That general store would become legendary even before the death of its owner. Here could be purchased horse collars or dill pickles, ground coffee or bib overalls, chewing tobacco or boots and shoes and paid for when and if the crops were threshed and in the warehouse. If it was a year of crop failure, and there were many such years, Simon Cohn would carry his farm customers for another year before receiving his money, and if the second year was also a failure, he would extend credit into the third. Most would pay in the end, but there would always be a few who could not, and some who would not, meet their obligations. It became legendary that Simon Cohn never foreclosed on a mortgage or unduly pressed his debtors. Those days of the pioneers were rough, and the merchant of the times had to be prepared to roll with the tides of prosperity and adversity. Simon would have the satisfaction of retaining the patronage of many of his old customers long after more modern stores became available to them in Oxnard. And if that was not enough to soothe the soul, there was always that bread box where one could sit and watch God's setting sun and the race of man passing his front porch with ever increasing speed.

It was the practice of carrying farmers over until harvest time that resulted in the most famous of all legends concerning Simon Cohn. The story has been told and retold over and over again, with each narrator changing, embellishing, or modifying the tale until no true account of what actually happened is now possible. Essentially the story was this:

One day during a rush period of business, a customer came into

Simon's store and purchased a saddle. The press of other business prevented Cohn from making out the usual sales note, and when closing time came, he was unable to remember who had bought the saddle. As time passed, and he was still at loss to recall the purchaser, Simon Cohn pondered the problem of how he was ever to collect the money. Then an idea came: He would bill all his customers for a new saddle. Those who had not purchased it would naturally call his attention to the error, while the real buyer would pay for the saddle.

At billing time (when the crops were in), Simon did just that, only to receive a remittance for the saddle from a large percentage of his customers. Precisely how many paid depends upon the particular storyteller, but the number is really inconsequential. The point that bothers this writer is that no one ever continues the tale to its logical conclusion.

If one analyzes the status of affairs, Simon Cohn was now in a worse predicament than before. As an honest merchant, he had collected X number of dollars to which he was not entitled and could not accept. What was worse, he still did not know the real purchaser of that saddle.

It is known that of all the stories told on the man, Simon Cohn liked the one about the saddle the best, but if he ever explained how he extricated himself from the dilemma, this writer has never heard any of the narrators of the tale give the answer. Nor has it ever been pointed out that Simon's customers were paying him a magnificent tribute by never questioning the honesty of his billings in the case. If Simon Cohn said they owed him for a saddle, they must have owed him for a saddle, and that was all there was to it.

There were times, of course, when a billing was questioned. Soon after Mr. Cohn opened his trading post at the Crossroads, a Mr. G.

W. Faulkner from Ohio purchased the seventy acres of land across Vineyard Avenue from Cohn's general store. Faulkner had need for some oats and made a deal with Mr. Cohn to take delivery of the grain, with the stipulation that he would make payment by a certain date at an agreed-upon price with the appropriate interest of the period added to the cost. In the interim grain prices rose sharply, and when payment time came, Faulkner received Cohn's bill for the oats, but at the increased price plus interest. Written on the bill were the words, "Adjusted by Simon Cohn." Faulkner drew a line through the adjustment note, made out a remittance for the original agreed-upon price plus interest, and added a note of his own: "Readjusted by G. W. Faulkner." That ended the matter.

Mr. Faulkner, like most of the pioneer farmers, was an excellent carpenter and blacksmith. On one occasion Simon Cohn hired him to construct some shelves in the store and do other repair work. The results were so pleasing to Mr. Cohn that he felt Faulkner was entitled to a bonus. Bringing forth "a drap o' the craythur," Simon said, "Here, Mr. Faulkner, have a drink on me."

"Why thank you, Mr. Cohn, but I don't drink."

Recovering from his astonishment to find someone in New Jerusalem that didn't drink, Simon withdrew and soon returned with the finest box of cigars in the store.

"Here, Mr. Faulkner, have a cigar."

"Why thank you, Mr. Cohn, but I don't smoke," Faulkner replied.

Simon Cohn looked unbelievingly at the man, and then observed with admiration, "Mr.

Faulkner, some day you will be well off."

Mr. Cohn was known to have loved music and prided himself upon being a good judge thereof. During the early 1880s, he purchased one of those popular instruments of day—a pump organ. Unpacking the bulky crate, Simon set up the organ in the post office portion of the general store, pulled out a few stops, and proceeded to test the instrument. Outside Riley Wooley had tied his team to the post office hitching post and gone inside for his mail. He was just in time to hear the postmaster's exclamation of delight over the superlative tone of the new organ.

Meanwhile, Wooley's team tied outside had other ideas in respect to the tonal attributes of that organ. They did not know precisely what the noise was that was emanating from the post office, but they were certain that New Jerusalem had never heard anything like it before. Simon Cohn proclaimed it "the finest toned organ in Ventura County," but the horses thought it sounded more like a Missouri mule responding to the mating call of a bull moose. Wooley emerged from the post office just in time to restore order and prevent the hitching post from being torn up by the roots.

Mr. Cohn's appreciation of fine music did not extend to the point of opening up his store when the Hueneme Brass Band cart over to serenade the Crossroads in 1884. The New Jerusalem correspondent noted that Hueneme was very fortunate that the band went out of town "to practice," and "it is rumored that one man who was sweetly serenaded gave them $5 to leave."

Of all the stories told on Simon Cohn—from the newspaper report that he was digging an artesian well to dilute a shipment of bitters that was causing too many jim-jam yells and Apache war whoops to the saddle story of later years—the favorite of this writer was told by Simon's son-in-law, George Zander.

The occasion was a special Elks Club event in Oxnard at which most of the living pioneers on the Colonia were present. It was a time for reminiscing, storytelling, and reliving those good old days of so long ago. If one could tell a yarn on another old-timer present at the party, so much the better. One pioneer, well advanced in years, got to his feet and facing Simon Cohn told the following tale:

"Simon, years ago I was in your store to buy a suit of clothes. There were two suits my size—one marked nine dollars and the other eleven dollars. I much preferred the eleven-dollar suit, and when you weren't looking, I changed the price tags and bought the eleven-dollar suit dollars suit for nine dollars."

The crowd roared its approval of the story, for there were few people who ever outsmarted the merchant of New Jerusalem. Then Simon Cohn rose slowly to his feet to respond.

"Well, that's a pretty good story, but, gentlemen, I'll tell you something: both those suits cost me six dollars!"

Yes, one had to get up very early if he expected to outsmart Simon Cohn, but it was great fun to try, and Simon enjoyed the sport as much as anyone. That was the way the pioneers played the game: a helping hand when needed, respect for the other fellow's rights, and a bit of western rawhiding thrown in to make life interesting, but one had to be able to "take it" as well as "dish it out." Simon Cohn could do both.

Anyone returning from Oxnard after November 16, 1936, would notice immediately that something was missing in El Rio. The familiar bread box on the front porch of Cohn's store was vacant. The little man in the dark suit and heavy glasses was no longer sitting there facing the west and watching the world go by. Simon Cohn's sun had set below the horizon, but the light of his life would shine on as long as men remembered and told stories of the pioneer days in Ventura County.

Chapter Three

EL RIO DEVELOPMENTS

1865–1870: Springville, the Place That Used to Be

RESIDENCE OF W. D. WOOD, SPRINGVILLE, VENTURA CO. CAL.

On the 101 freeway south of El Rio, you will find an off ramp named Springville. This was where the old settlement of Springville used to be. The Homestead Act of 1862 brought migrants to California and Santa Barbara county in search of farmland. Public land was scarce, particularly because many ranchos had not been patented at this time. Hearings were held over the ownership of these lands. These lands were made available for homesteading, and one portion became the site of the small community of Springville. It was named after a large spring that was located there.

By 1878 there were two general stores, a blacksmith shop, a hotel, a restaurant and two feed stables. When the railroad reached Saticoy in 1887, Springville lost part of its business. With the opening of the sugar beet factory in Oxnard in 1898, most of the residents picked up their homes and establishments and moved there for employment opportunities. Finally, with the establishment of Camarillo, Springville reached its end. Even the Springville cemetery was removed. The Springville area is currently experiencing large developments. It is mentioned here due to its proximity to El Rio and because El Rio also experienced the same type of exodes of its residents at that time.

1877: The Santa Clara Chapel

The Santa Clara Chapel was built in 1877, years before the Santa Clara church in downtown Oxnard. A May 10, 1979, article in the *Marina & Tower Views* reported it was built by Jewish merchant

Simon Cohn for his Mexican and Spanish speaking customers and neighbors. And that it still stood at that time but was moved to the Colonia area, which was not correct. It was the first church in the Santa Clara valley.

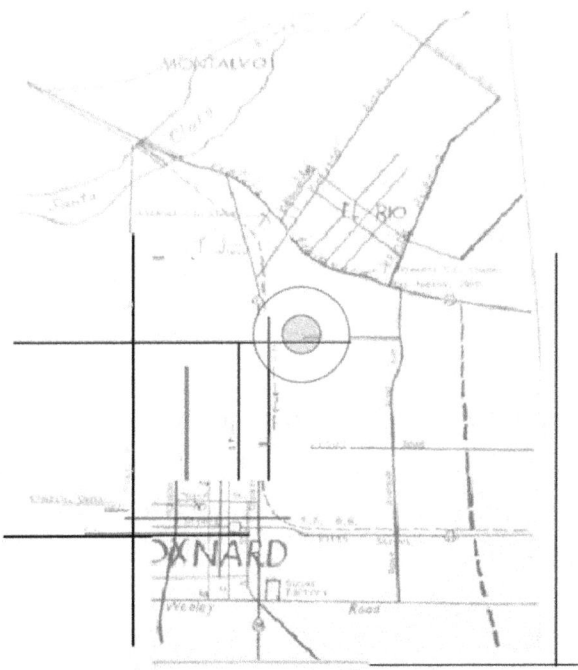

It originally was located at the west end of Colonia Avenue at Ventura Boulevard, later called Myrtle Street in El Rio. It was moved to its current location on Rose Avenue due to the buildout of the 101 freeway in the early 1950s. However, in 1989 a plaque was erected next to Tilly's at the Esplanade stating that that was where the chapel was located. That cannot be correct either as in discussing this matter with remaining El Rio elders (who were in their 90s), who attended that chapel, all have confirmed that it was at the end of Colonia Avenue where Krispy Cream currently is. Also in a book published around 1989 called *A Tower in the Valley (A History of the Santa Clara Church)*, there is a map clearly showing the chapel was at the corner of Colonia Avenue and Myrtle Street. I leave it up to the reader to draw their own conclusions.

1882: The Post Office

The US Postal Service established the New Jerusalem Post Office on July 26, 1882, and Simon Cohn was appointed the first postmaster. The name was later shortened to Jerusalem. On February 14, 1895, the postal authority changed the name to El Rio, which means the river. Four months later they changed it to Elrio, one word. Then they changed it back to El Rio. Eventually the post office was finally discontinued on October 31, 1911.

There is no photo of the El Rio post office. However, this is a photo of the post office in the town of Harmony Ca. It was built in 1866 and gives an idea of what the El Rio post office may have looked like.

1885: El Rio School District

The Rio School District was established in 1885. It is not known how many students attended, whether it had two, four, six, or eight, but it did not exceed thirteen. The first school was located one mile north of the town center on the Schiappa Prieta Ranch. That site was also known as the Old Cactus Patch. A few years later, it was moved about three blocks west to the corner of Vineyard Avenue and Stroube Street. In 1895 a new two-acre school site was purchased on that property for $400 in gold coins. The building had a dome-shaped roof on its bell tower.

It contained four classrooms, and a large center hall that was also used as a classroom. In 1948 a ten-acre site was purchased, and plans for that new El Rio school were completed in 1949. This site is on Vineyard Avenue across Sycamore Street on El Rio Lane. The school consisted of nine classrooms, one kindergarten, and one-half administration building for all elementary grades. In 1952 five additional classrooms were added and the following year additional classrooms, a multipurpose room, nurses, and kitchen alterations were added as well as a book and teachers' room. What transpired after this is covered under the Martinez family chapter. That school was demolished in June 2024 to make way for a planned 167 condominium complex.

1885: The Oxnard's and the Sugar Beets

A May 10, 1979, article states that in the 1880s, Oxnard did not exist, and Hueneme was just a spot on the coast. Around 1885 two out-of-state brothers came to Simon Cohn with the idea of buying land to build a sugar-beet factory. Simon turned them down as he felt sugar-beet processing would contaminate the natural agricultural area.

The Oxnard brothers had to go someplace else, and they did. They completed their factory in south Oxnard in August 1898. This caused an uprooting of people in El Rio and the township of Springville, which was south of Nyeland Acres. Many people picked up their houses and moved to Oxnard for the new jobs created by the new beet factory. The city of Oxnard was finally incorporated in 1903.

1898: The Montalvo Bridge

The crossroads at Vineyard Avenue and Ventura Boulevard was also a junction. This is where people heading toward Ventura or Los Angeles could stop to rest or have a drink or two or three of

Johnny Walker or Gordon gin to drown the memories of the bumpy stagecoach ride from where they came from. There was no bridge over the Santa Clara river until 1898. Until then travelers had to drive their stagecoaches and horses through the river, and it had to be done when the water level was low, or you did not make it. Many people died trying to ford the river. When the bridge was built, it was called the Montalvo Bridge and is now part of the 101 freeway over that river.

1921: El Rio Boxing and Wrestling Stadium

In 1921 Simon Cohn built the El Rio American sports stadium, which hosted boxing and wrestling bouts. It was built behind a garage that was opposite Cohn's store somewhere near the Financial Tower. It was an open-air 1,500-seat arena suitable for boxing and wrestling events. It had four hundred ringside seats, a hundred on four sides. Bleachers were behind the reserved chairs with one main entrance and four exits with ample parking. A roof was built later. It had a few name changes such as the El Rio Legion Arena or the El Rio Arena. The total cost was $5,000. Opening day was September 9, 1921. Events were held there for thirty years until 1954 when it was demolished to make way for the 101 freeway buildout. Photos of the arena itself have not been found, but wrestling ads have been provided.

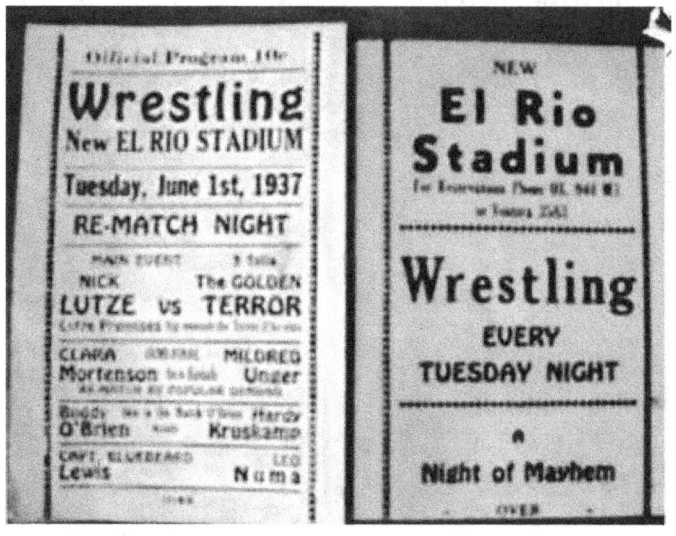

1923: Teatro Luz

The Villegas family established the area's first movie theater, Teatro Luz, in 1923, at the corner of Olive Street and Colonia Avenue. It also had a grocery store. The silent movie theater brought movies such as *Sign of the Cross*, *The Lone Star Ranger*, *Ben Hur*, and movies featuring cowboy stars Tom Mix and William S. Hart. The family lived next door. Some of our elders remember going to those movies at 7:30 p.m. Sunday nights, and the Villegas girls sold tickets (kids ten cents and adults fifteen cents). They sold homemade popcorn and soda pop. And they also had raffles and live musical entertainment. Unfortunately the theater closed down in 1929 after the talkies and the depression came in. There is much more Villegas information in chapter four.

1941: US Department of Agriculture

Farm Security Administration Farmworkers Community

In June 1941, although it is not stated where exactly in El Rio this was, a migrant farmworker camp was set up by the Department of Agriculture. It consisted of tents and shacks where those migrants lived while they worked the fields. The spiritual needs of these residents were attended to by Father Garcia of the Catholic church.

1945: Prisoner of War Camp

Photo courtesy of **Jeffrey Geiger**
SIMILAR SETTING: The Camp Cooke branch camp near Saticoy likely looked much like this one in Agus Ranch near Tulare.

In 1945 during World War II, a prisoner of war camp holding about five hundred German prisoners from Europe and Africa was set up at the corner of Vineyard and Central Avenues where the current Red Wing boot store is in the Strickland area of El Rio. Camp Cooke was located in Lompoc where Vandenberg Airforce base is today. Camp Cooke had sixteen branches, and this was one of them. So the eighteen acres in El Rio were chosen for the camp. Ranchers paid $100,000 to build the camp due to the success of using German prisoners to harvest crops.

The area had not been developed yet, so the captives were housed in Quonset huts. The farmers, in order not to make waves, decided to keep it out of the press. The prisoners were put to work picking lemons and oranges for farmers in Saticoy. The prisoners were housed and treated better than the Mexican workers here at the time. The camp closed down in the spring of 1946.

1951–1954: The 101 Freeway

It is important to note the biggest impact on El Rio occurred from 1951 to 1954 when the 101 freeway came through the area. This would result in the removal of Cohn's store as well as his boxing ring. It also caused the removal of the Santa Clara Chapel to Rose Avenue and Ventura Boulevard. The state had Ventura Boulevard realigned west toward Cortez Street (twice).

Eminent domain was initiated resulting in the removal of residents' homes. The state did not pay the amounts these properties were worth, resulting in unfair taking of personal property, but nothing was ever done.

1966: Los Compadres del Rio

LOS COMPADRES DEL RIO

OFFICERS

Richard Maria	President
Jess Velasquez	Vice President
Ernest Almanza	Secretary
Charles Gonzales	Treasurer
Henry Luna	Public Relations and Historian
Roy Coronado	Sergeant-At-Arms

CHARTERED JANUARY 24, 1966

Briefly, why the Los Compadres Club was organized

To establish a Scholarship Fund to assist higher education or Mexican-American students; to aid and encourage the development of youth; to promote an active interest in good government and Civic affairs; to inspire respect for law; to promote Patriotism and work for Inter-National accord among all people.

MEMBERS

Almanza, Ernest J.
Almanza, Louie
Cervantes, Benjamin
Chacon, John
Coronado, Roy
Gonzales, Charles
Guillen, Robert
Lerma, Frank
Lopez, Robert
Luna, Henry
Maria, Richard
Martinez, Albert
Perez, John
Reyes, Tony
Rocha, Louie
Sabedra, Frank
Vasquez, Billy
Velasquez, Jess
Velasquez, Pascual

A November 12, 1967, article highlights the placement of rain gutters on Colonia Avenue by the El Rio service club called Los Compadres

(Godfathers) del Rio. They are described as a lively group of men. These were twenty-two men whose goals included the betterment of higher education and the development of good civic affairs.

They held barbecues to raise funds to help the boys & girls who went to Rio Mesa High school. The surnames of these members included Ayala, Martinez, Velasquez, Sabedra, Luna, Maria, Almanza, Miller, Perez, Reyes, Chacon, Lerma, Macias, Rocha, Ledesma, Segovia, and others. This included World War II veterans. Their families still live in El Rio.

They also constructed the gutters along Colonia Avenue in 1967. And yes, of course the wives and families of these and other members did the cooking and serving at the picnics and barbeques they sponsored while the guys did the work. In those days all these families had each other's backs. A tradition seemingly lost in the march of time.

The January-February 1969 Flood of Ventura County

A 1969 booklet called *The Great Flood of Ventura County* describes the disasters caused by the storms of January and February 1969. Among these the Santa Clara River teetered on the brink of being breached where the Collection and Riverpark now are, which would have flooded El Rio. Also included was the destruction of the Saticoy bridge and many other disasters and deaths brought on by this catastrophe.

Chapter Four

PORTRAITS EL RIO PIONEERS

Although there were other families in El Rio, the following are highlighted due to the times they arrived after the county of Ventura was created and the results of their businesses and other efforts to bring substantial and positive changes to our township. We need to know and remember where they came from.

1870: Anselmo "Cap" Ruiz

Anselmo "Cap" Ruiz was considered the unofficial mayor and number one citizen of El Rio. He was born on April 17, 1870, in Santa Barbara. Ventura County had not been established yet, so this was still Santa Barbara at that time. He passed away on July 19, 1971, at 101 years old. His July 21, 1971, obituary stated that he died at an Oxnard Hospital (St. John's) after a brief illness. It stated that his grandparents were early settlers in the Santa Barbara area.

He was a long-time employee of the Hobson ranch and proprietor of a store in El Rio for many years. He also tended the water tanks of the El Rio Mutual Water Company, which were located on his property behind his house at 2607 Colonia Avenue.

As unofficial mayor, local citizens and political candidates sought his guidance in personal and political matters. For his one hundredth birthday, four streets in El Rio were roped off, and a celebration was held in his honor. That day was proclaimed Cap Ruiz Day by the county board of supervisors, and he received congratulatory messages from high officials, including President Nixon and Governor Ronald Reagan.

He was survived by his wife, Yola, and several nieces and nephews. A rosary was recited at 7:30 p.m. that Friday at James A. Reardon Mortuary ,and a requiem mass was celebrated at 8:30 a.m. that Saturday in the Santa Clara church. The burial was at the Santa Clara cemetery.

1875: Simon Cohn

As previously mentioned, Simon Cohn was a Jewish German immigrant who settled in El Rio in 1875, two years after Ventura County was created. In 1879 Colonel J. D. Hines, the county's first superior court judge, dubbed the place New Jerusalem in reference to the Jewish ownership of the area. But the name was never officially recognized, although it was placed on Cohn's store.

Cohn was a general merchant, building and opening his store at the site that would eventually be called Four Corners at Vineyard Avenue and Ventura Boulevard across from where the current McDonald's is. Cohn's home was built behind his store.

Cohn's holdings extended from the Santa Clara River to Rice Road and from Oxnard Boulevard to the Strickland area at Central Avenue where Rio Mesa High School is. His holdings also included the Wagon Wheel and Esplanade areas. He is known to have built the little Catholic Santa Clara chapel, which was originally located at the corner of Colonia Avenue and Myrtle streets.

1886: John Donlon

John Donlon Sr. was not a native of El Rio or California for that matter. He was born in 1846 and migrated from Ireland to the United States around 1870. He first resided in New York and San Francisco. Thereafter he worked in San Jose and Alameda before moving to El Rio. In 1886 Donlon bought 403 acres of land and initiated his own ranch. The ranch was located where the Riverpark communities and the  Collection shopping centers are today. It ran north of the 101 freeway from the Esplanade all the way up to Stroube Street. His ranch involved keeping livestock such as sheep, cattle, and pigs and growing crops such as lima beans, grains, alfalfa and barley.

An important discovery was made when plowing near the river bottom of the Santa Clara River. The plow struck an object that turned out to be a six-pound cannon thought to have been buried by John C. Fermont's troops as they made their way south from Ventura during the war between Mexico and the United States in 1847.

On June 24, 1886, he married Mary Forrer, a native of Utah. The Forrers moved to El Rio where Mary went to work for Donlon's cousin Pete doing housework and cleaning. They were the first couple married in the El Rio chapel Simon Cohn built.

This union produced twelve children: Peter, William, Clara, Theresa, John, Kathryn, Lawrence, Mary, Ida, Nazarene, Morgan, and Donlon Jr. The Donlons were proud of raising their family in El Rio because it was a good community with good neighbors. It was home, and they were proud to live there. John Donlon Sr. served forty years on the El Rio school board. This family along with the Donlon cousins of Oxnard made many positive developments to our area.

1899: The Villegas

Arturo Villegas "financed" El Rio's fir movie house.

It was 1899 when the Villegas family from a mining town called Guadalupe in Zacatecas, Mexico, arrived in El Rio (New Jerusalem). This included Mama Lupe, Micaela, and Luis. They brought two daughters, Sara and Ester, and three sons, Arthur, Luis, and Antonio.

This was an enterprising family who came to California by the promise of golden opportunities. This family built Teatro Luz on the corner of Colonia Avenue and Olive Street in El Rio. They not only positively affected El Rio, but they also helped create Oxnard and Hueneme.

They started the area's first taxicab company. They drafted construction designs, plans and prints for the port of Hueneme, and constructed businesses in Oxnard such as Herrera's Market, Munoz Billiards, and La Inglesia Apostolica on Cooper Road in La Colonia.

1915–1916: The Velasquezes

After the start of the Mexican Revolution, many families had to leave Mexico due to the threat to their lives. Such was the case of the Velasquez family of Leon Guanajuato who arrived in California around 1915/1916. They actually laid family footprints in both Pacoima in the San Fernando Valley and in El Rio. Severiano, born in 1870, and Francisca Lira Velasquez, born in 1871, brought their family members with them to El Rio. These members were Anastacio (Tacho), Adolpho, Mike, Martina, and Catarina. Severiano had been foremen of an area called the Sandia. They established homes on Colonia Avenue.

Tacho married Lila Solano in 1920. Adolfo's wife was Francisca, Mike's wife was Grace, Martina's husband was Pillar Sabedra, and

Catarina's husband was Marcos Miller. The children of these unions not only resulted in marriages and families of the Velasquezes and Sabedras but also the Lunas, the Rochas, and the Marias.

Adolpho and Mike worked for years as caretakers at Ivy Lawn cemetery. Mike's kids included Al, Clara, Froylan, Gene, Adeline, and Estella. Adolpho's children were Bonnie, Gonio, Lon, Lupe, Rickie, Mary, and Kelo. Adolpho built a pool hall on Colonia Avenue. During its construction they discovered a human skeleton buried on the site. His daughter Bonnie told me before she passed away at one hundred years old that they used to make their own liquor at the site during prohibition. His daughter Ricky married Ralph Luna who operated construction/trucking businesses.

Martina Sabedra's children were Ben, Mino, Joe, Cruz, Lala, Kiko, Daniel, and Lassito.

One of Martina's sons (Ben) established his wife Ramona's store and Estill's bar on Cortez Street and Ventura Boulevard. Lala Sabedra married Louie Rocha who operated his vehicle repair shop across the street, which is still in use today at the corner of Cortez Street and Ventura Boulevard. Lala will be one hundred years old in December 2024. Ben's brother Joe (Chepe) was a medic in the Pacific Theater of World War II from 1942 to 1945 and then worked for the city of Oxnard until he retired. He passed away at one hundred years old.

Catarina's husband Marcos Miller passed away at the age of thirty-three in 1933. They had three children: Mary, Bernardo, and Cora Miller. Bernardo passed away at one and a half years old. Mary married Henry Olivas who was killed in a collision with a train in 1952. Cora married Richard Maria, and she is still with us today as are Ricky Luna, Lala Rocha, and Daniel Sabedra.

1921: The Martinezes

Frank and Andrea Martinez pose in front of their El Rio market, says Frank, "I was raised here it has a lot of sentimental value."

Jesus (1892) and Jescita (1893) Martinez were from Durango, Mexico, and arrived in El Rio in 1921. They had eighteen children consisting of Randy, Gene, Roger, Hortencia, Chavela, Frank, Ramiro, Eva, Martha, Alice, Freddy, Mary, Rose, Connie, and Eddie. Don Jesus Martinez came with the dream of making a better life for his family. He found a job working for Simon Cohn in his store where he learned the ropes of a general merchant. The kids were put to work to help the family.

The old El Rio school located at Vineyard Avenue and Stroube Street was being auctioned off by the district. Don Jesus put his bid in and obtained the site. Joe Ramirez, who had married Cruz Sabedra, was commissioned to build the large brick building that became Martinez Market at the corner of Stroube Street and Vineyard Avenue. That market still operates today.

However, the school building itself was not demolished but recycled into small apartments, a large storage building, and two smaller businesses that are still there today. This was and is El Rio's business district after the 101 buildout removed the district Cohn had developed.

The school replacing the old one was built a couple of blocks south on Vineyard Avenue.

Sadly that school had been shuttered and was demolished in 2024 to make way for the development of condominiums and a business building. One of the remaining Martinez sons, Freddy, provided valuable historical information to this writer regarding El Rio and the citizens who lived and worked toward the betterment of our community as did all these families.

The Business Districts

An August 1966 article called "El Rio: Rural Living in a Community Once Called New Jerusalem," shares some history of New Jerusalem with photos of the Bank of A. Levy in the town's business district on the corner of Vineyard Avenue and Stroube Street. It is still there. Also included are photos of an old saloon at Myrtle Street and Vineyard Avenue. The article stated that New Jerusalem is now buried directly under the Vineyard overpass. With the northbound traffic going over Simon Cohn's general store and the Silver Pitcher Saloon. Buried here too is the sports arena Simon had built that hosted boxing and wrestling matches back in the day.

El Rio's old business district that Cohn developed disappeared due to the 101 freeway. It relocated to the areas of Vineyard Avenue, Stroube Street, and Collins Avenue. Now that current business is being redeveloped for residential uses.

Epilogue

In the end it is hoped that El Rio is not swallowed up completely by development as has happened with the Esplanade, the Collection, Wagon Wheel, and now the El Rio School. It's ironic that the city the Oxnard Brothers founded after Simon Cohn sent them on their way over a hundred years ago has come back to our little slice of heaven called New Jerusalem.

Tidbits to Remember

The Santa Clara River was originally named Rio de Santa Clara on August 9, 1769, by the Portola expedition on the march north from San Diego to establish a mission in Monterey. It was named in honor of Saint Clare of Assisi who died on August 11, 1253. In essence our area went from being the Chumash lands of the Muwu and Lisiqishi tribes to being renamed Rancho Santa Clara Del Norte, then Centreville, then New Jerusalem in 1875, and finally El Rio.

It is a surprising fact and mostly unknown to our residents that the little Catholic chapel was provided by a Prussian Jew. For that we must be grateful.

The following are the dates that each of the cities in Ventura County were founded or incorporated. The city of Ventura was founded in 1782 along with the mission and incorporated in 1866.

The county of Ventura was established in 1873. Santa Paula was founded in 1872 and incorporated in 1902. Ojai was founded in 1866. Oxnard was incorporated in 1903. Fillmore in 1914. Port Hueneme in 1948, Camarillo in 1964, Thousand Oaks in 1964, Simi Valley in 1969, and finally Moorpark in 1983.

Acknowledgments

The author would like to thank the following for their advice, encouragement and support; Jeffery Wayne Maulhardt, Maria Villegas Navarez, Freddy Martinez, Angie Oretta and Mario (Mando) A. Riley Jr.

www.ingramcontent.com/pod-product-compliance
Lightning Source LLC
LaVergne TN
LVHW012036060526
838201LV00061B/4628